I0459272

In the interest of reaching every truth-seeking mind that desires to escape the path that leads to destruction of both body and soul, this tract will be distributed free of charge as long as the issue lasts.

TRACT NO. 1

Second Revised Edition

The Universal Publishing Assn.
P.O. Box 24027
Waco, Texas 76702

UniversalPublishing.com
ISBN: 978-1-962573-08-5

PRINTED IN U.S.A.

PREFACE

Personally Watching for Every Ray of Light.

One who entrusts to another the investigation of a message from the Lord, is making flesh his arm, and thus is foolishly acting as without a mind of his own. And "the mind that depends upon the judgment of others is certain, sooner or later, to be misled."—*Education*, p. 231.

Similarly, one who allows prejudice to bar him from a candid investigation of anything new, coming in the name of the Lord, is unwittingly an infidel.

Likewise he who is satisfied with his present attainments in the Word of God, says in effect: "I am rich, and increased with goods, and have need of nothing."

All these, in variously acting out the part which provoked the condemnation written against the Laodiceans, thereby fulfilling the prophecy which they ought not fulfill, are preparing themselves to be spued out (Rev. 3:14-18). And if they continue in their self-satisfied attitude that they have all the truth, and so have need of nothing more, they will spurn every new claimant to truth and toss the message into the discard because it comes through an unexpected channel. Certainly, then, were this tract not the unfolding of prophecy, the fact is inevitable that when the unfoldment did come, they would treat it in like manner, and consequently toss away their salvation!

Throughout the ages, all who have put their trust in the so-called wise men, and foremost Christians of the day, all reputedly godly men, have by these very ones been bereft of the crown of eternal life, as were the Jewish laity in the days of Christ because of their failing to assume full responsibility for their own salvation. Presumptuously trusting in the wisdom of their so-called "great men," they declined to believe in Christ's words: "O Father, Lord of heaven and earth, . . . Thou hast *hid* these things from the *wise* and prudent, and hast revealed them unto babes." Matt. 11:25. "Where is the wise? where is the scribe? . . . hath not God made foolish the wisdom of this world?" 1 Cor. 1:20.

". . . if a message comes that you do not understand, take pains that you may hear the reasons the messenger may give, comparing scripture with scripture, that you may know whether or not it is sustained by the Word of God."—*Testimonies on Sabbath-School Work*, p. 65.

Will you not, therefore, Brother, Sister, cease to copy the mistakes of others? Will you not profit by them? If you will, you are duty-bound to use your own mind in reaching for salvation, lest you fail to understand the saving truth in the momentous exposé, the

Pre-"Eleventh Hour" Extra! The Dardanelles of the Bible.

The call of Ezekiel to the prophetic office is one of the most interesting experiences of the ancient seers, and the revelation of what he saw by the river Chebar is perhaps of greater importance to heaven and earth at this time than is any other vision on sacred record, because in a remarkable way it reveals That Which unites Heaven with Earth, even as the Dardanelles links two important seas. Thus, this study of Ezekiel's vision, which brings to light earth's being visited by the Majesty of the Universe, may be aptly termed, "The Dardanelles of the Bible."

The reader who would best comprehend this seemingly most confusing and complicated of Bible symbolisms, will follow the cover-page objectification, in conjunction with

The Prophet's Description of the Mysteries Herein Treated.

"And I looked, and, behold, a whirlwind came out of the north, a great cloud, and a fire infolding itself, and a brightness was about it, and out of the midst thereof as the colour of amber, out of the midst of the fire.

"Also out of the midst thereof came the likeness of four living creatures. And this was their appearance; they had the likeness of a man. And every one had four faces, and every one had four wings. And their feet were straight feet; and the sole of their feet was like the sole of a calf's foot: and they sparkled like the colour of burnished brass. And they had the hands of a man under their wings on their four sides; and they four had their faces and their wings. Their wings were joined one to another; they turned not when they went; they went every one straight forward.

"As for the likeness of their faces, they four had the face of a man, and the face of a lion, on the right side: and they four had the face of an ox on the left side; they four also had the face of an eagle. . . . "And I saw as the colour of amber, as the appearance of fire round about within it, from the appearance of his loins even upward, and from the appearance of his loins even downward, I saw as it were the appearance of fire, and it had brightness round about. As the appearance of the bow that is in the cloud in the day of rain, so was the appearance of the brightness round about. This was the appearance of the likeness of the glory of the Lord. And when I saw it, I fell upon my face, and I heard a voice of one that spake." Ezek. 1:4-10, 27, 28.

"And it came to pass, that when He had commanded *the man* clothed with linen, saying, Take fire from between the wheels, from between the cherubims; then he went in, and stood beside the wheels." Ezek. 10:6.

To this marvelous scene which Ezekiel saw on the river bank in the land of the Chaldeans, our undivided attention is now called. Being "the appearance of the likeness of the glory of the Lord," obviously, then, it was

The Lord on One of His Thrones.

Besides this divine appearance which Ezekiel saw (Ezek. 1:28), the Bible describes God enthroned on three other occasions—once as seen by Isaiah, and twice as seen by John the Revelator; to wit:

(1) ". . . I saw also the Lord sitting upon a throne, high and lifted up, and His train filled the temple. *Above* it stood the *seraphims*: each one had six wings; with twain he covered his face, and with twain he covered his feet, and with twain he did fly. And one cried unto another, and said, Holy, holy, holy, is the Lord of hosts: the whole earth is full of His glory. And the posts of the door moved at the voice of him that cried and the house was filled with smoke." Isa. 6:1-4.

(2) "And immediately I was in the spirit: and, behold, a throne was set in heaven, and one sat on the throne . . . And round about the throne were four and twenty seats: and upon the seats I saw four and twenty elders sitting, clothed in white raiment; and they had on their heads

crowns of gold . . . and there were seven lamps of fire burning before the throne, which are the seven Spirits of God. And before the throne there was a sea of glass like unto crystal: and in the midst of the throne, and round about the throne, were four beasts full of eyes before and behind." Rev. 4:2, 4-6.

(3) "And he shewed me a pure river of water of life, clear as crystal, proceeding out of the throne of God and of the Lamb." Rev. 22:1.

Since the throne seen by Isaiah was a *"train"* (retinue), and since as it entered into the temple, "the posts of the door moved at the voice of him that cried, and the house was filled with smoke" (Isa. 6:1, 4), it therefore is a traveling throne, whereas both the one of Revelation 4, having the *"sea of glass"* before it, and the one of Revelation 22, having the *"river . . . of life"* before it, are stationary thrones.

Though the one which Ezekiel saw, is similar to the one which Isaiah was shown, yet they are distinct and separate thrones, for each of the "seraphims" of Isaiah's vision has *six wings*, while each of the "cherubims" of Ezekiel's vision has but *four*. In the latter, moreover, the cherubims stood under the throne, whereas in the former, they stood above it. On record, therefore, are four thrones—two stationary, and two traveling.

In determining the location of the throne of Revelation 4, and the one of Revelation 22, we note to begin with that the latter, the one from which the "river . . . of life" proceeds, is, says the Revelator, "the throne of God and of the *Lamb*"—that upon which Christ sat at the right hand of God after His resurrection. The former, the one having the sea of glass before it, is (also according to John's view) in the most holy apartment of the heavenly sanctuary, for John saw before it "seven lamps of fire" (Rev. 4:5) — a sanctuary fixture. "As in vision the apostle John was granted a view of the temple of God in heaven, he beheld there 'seven lamps of fire burning before the throne.' "— *The Great Controversy,* p. 414.

Then, concerning the Father and the Son's moving from the throne of God and of the Lamb—the one where the river of life is—to the throne where the sea of glass is, we read: "I saw the *Father rise from the throne,* and in a flaming chariot go into the holy of holies *within the vail*, and sit down. *Then Jesus rose up from the* throne, . . . Then a cloudy chariot, with wheels like flaming fire, surrounded by angels, came to where Jesus was. He stepped into the chariot and was borne to the holiest, where the Father sat."—*Early Writings*, p 55.

Recording the same event as he saw it, Daniel says: "I beheld till the thrones were cast down, and the Ancient of days did sit, Whose garment was white as snow, and the hair of His head like the pure wool: His throne was like the fiery flame, and His wheels as burning fire. A fiery stream issued and came forth from before Him: thousand thousands ministered unto Him, and ten thousand times ten thousand stood before Him: the judgment was set, and the books were opened." Dan. 7:9, 10.

Our greatest interest, however, at this point, is to know the location and the mission of the throne which Ezekiel saw, and concerning which he says: ". . . I looked, and, behold, a whirlwind came out of the north." Ezek. 1:4. The fact that the "whirlwind," enveloping the throne, "came," says Ezekiel, shows that this throne, just as with the one of Isaiah 6, is a moving one, and that it came to the banks of the river Chebar.

"This is the living creature," continues Ezekiel, "that I saw under the God of Israel [Who is "above the cherubims"], by the river of Chebar; and I knew that they were the cherubims." "And the cherubims lifted up their wings, and mounted up from the earth in my sight." Ezek. 10:20, 19.

As the chariot's mounting "up from the earth" shows that in this particular throne, God visits the earth and then, when His mission is accomplished, returns to heaven, naturally our uppermost desire is to know the answer to the question,

According to Ezekiel 2:3; 3:1, 4, 5, 7, the prophet was to bear his message to the whole "house of Israel" (the term "house of Israel," denoting either all twelve tribes or only the ten tribes as the case might be). Yet he did not understand the meaning of the vision. Had he, he would have explained it, rather than declaring: "I came to them of the captivity at Telabib, that dwelt by the river of Chebar, and I sat where they sat, and remained there *astonished* among them seven days." Ezek. 3:15.

Since at the time of the vision, the house of Judah, the two-tribe kingdom, was in captivity in the land of the Chaldeans, and the house of Israel, the ten-tribe kingdom, was in dispersion among the nations whither it had been carried away and scattered some years before (2 Kings 17:6), there was no possibility of Ezekiel's delivering the message to them. And as it is to both the house of *Israel* and the house of *Judah* (Ezek. 9:9),—the twelve tribes,—consequently it was prophetic in Ezekiel's time.

The Jewish nation, moreover, up to the time of Christ, had no light on this prophecy, and it appeared to them as too complicated to understand, and even unsafe for an ordinary mind to read. "All this chapter appeared so obscure and full of mysteries, to the ancient Hebrews, that, as we learn from St. Jerome (*Ep. ad Paulin.,*) they suffered none to read it before they were thirty years old." *Douay* Version, footnote to Ezekiel 1:5. And having seen no light in this scripture until the present time, the Christian church has made little or no attempt to explain it.

And finally as no slaughter such as the one described in Ezekiel 9 has ever occurred, its fulfilment is obviously yet future.

Plainly, therefore, the vision *was prophetic* in Ezekiel's time, and has been prophetic ever since. And if it is ever to be fulfilled, and not remain a useless and unprofitable writing,—a thing which God never creates,—then its mystery must, of course, now be unveiled, and its action executed in the near future.

In the clear light of these facts, chapter nine is seen to hold the climactic scene of the vision. Describing the awful work which the Lord is to do when, with the cherubim, He visits the earth, it shows the fearsome consequences to those who reject its message: its blessings missed, the kingdom lost! Tragic, frightful experience, it shall be the fate of all who refuse now to awake and to know about it, but who choose rather to remain in ignorance of its truth, and of

The Object of the Lord's Coming In His Throne.

As the prophet was looking toward the north, he saw a "great cloud" coming like a "whirlwind" to earth. Watching with in-tense inter-est its drawing nearer and nearer, finally he saw the "living creatures," the "wheels," and the rest,—"the appearance of the likeness of the glory of the Lord." Whereupon, "I fell," he says, "upon my face, and I heard a *voice* of one that spake [unmistakably the Lord Himself come to give a message to Ezekiel].

". . . And He said unto me, Son of man, I send thee to the children of Israel, to a rebellious nation that hath rebelled against Me: they and their fathers have transgressed against Me, even unto this very day. For they are impudent children and stiff-heart-ed. I do send thee unto them; and thou shalt say unto them, Thus saith the Lord God. And they, whether they will hear, or whether they will forbear, (for they are a rebellious house,) yet shall know that there hath been a prophet among them. And thou, son of man, be not afraid of them, neither be afraid of their words, though briars and thorns be with thee, and thou dost dwell among scorpions: be not afraid of their words, nor be dismayed at their looks, though they be a re-bellious house." Ezek. 1:28; 2:3-6.

"And He said unto me," continues the prophet, "Son of man, go, get thee unto *the house of Israel*, and speak with My words unto them. For thou art not sent to a people of a strange speech and of an hard language, . . . whose words thou canst not under-stand." Ezek. 3:4-6.

These mandatory words (of weighty significance to all) reveal that the message which the prophet received is only for God's people, and that therefore, by logical extension, the entire vision, of which it is a part, meets its fulfilment at a time in which the Lord sends forth the warning that because His church is at a very low ebb spiritually,—"impudent and hard-hearted" and "a rebellious house,"—He will do within it a work of marking and slaying. And in all the Bible there is to be found in but one church a situation as to condition, cause, time, and result answering to that of the prophecy, and that is in

The Laodicean Church.

The condemnation of Rev. 3:14-18 against the Laodiceans, and the condemnation of Ezek. 2:1-7 and 3:4-7 against "the house of Israel," being the same, each therefore is the complement of the other: the one being the Revelation of that of which the other is the prophecy.

Both vindicate the *Spirit of Prophecy's* warning that no "greater deception can come upon human minds than a confidence that they are right, when they are all wrong! The message of the True Witness finds the people of God in a sad deception [instead of in an excellent condition], yet honest in that deception. They know not that their condition is deplorable in the sight of God. While those addressed are flattering themselves that they are in an

—14—

exalted spiritual condition, the *message* of the True Witness breaks their security by the startling denunciation of their true condition of spiritual blindness, poverty, and wretchedness. The testimony, so cutting and severe, *cannot be a mistake*, for it is the True Witness who speaks, and His testimony must be correct."—*Testimonies*, Vol. 3, pp. 252, 253.

Since the Lord says that "all the house of Israel are impudent and hardhearted" (Ezek. 3:7), then, certainly, will each one intent upon being saved, "determine to know the worst of" his "case" (*Testimonies*, Vol. 1, p. 163), and

The Time of the Church's Low Ebb.

Were God's people to continue self-deceived, "impudent and hardhearted," and were the spirituality of the church to continue to dim away, then with such a church the Lord could never finish His work on earth, and probation must finally close upon a world in utter darkness, having no living saints to translate at the appearing of Christ.

"The Lord does not *now* work," says the *Spirit of Prophecy,* "to bring many souls into the truth, because of the church-members who have never been converted, and those who were once converted but who have backslidden. What influence would these unconsecrated members have on new converts? Would they not make of no effect the God-given message which His people are to bear?"— *Id.,* Vol. 6, p. 371.

Having up till this time been holding back because of the unconverted and backslidden members in the church, what will He do now when, as He says, "*all* the house of Israel are impudent and hardhearted"? The very fact that He is holding back, is the most portentous evidence that He must do a special work for the church before it can finish His work upon earth.

Face to face with this solemn certainty, each one, therefore, who seeks "an inheritance on high," will maintain the strictest integrity and openness of mind as he studies concerning the special work involved, lest for his Laodicean affliction, He never find

The Remedy:

". . . *While the investigative judgment* is going forward in heaven, . . . there is to be a *special* work of *purification,* of putting away of sin, among God's people upon earth. . . . *Then* the church which our Lord at His coming is to receive to Himself will be 'a glorious church, *not having* spot, or wrinkle, or any such thing.' Then she will look forth 'as the morning, fair as the moon, clear as the sun, and terrible as an army with banners.' " "*Clad* in the armor of *Christ's righteousness*, the church is to enter upon her *final* conflict. . . . she is to go forth into *all* the world, *conquering* and to conquer."—*The Great Controversy*, p. 425; *Prophets and Kings*, p. 725.

Mark the italicized words: "*not having* spot," "her *final* conflict," "going forth into *all* the world, *conquering* and to conquer." These statements emphasize a pure and triumphant church, perfected by a "special work of purification" which must take place before the work of the gospel is finished in any part of the world.

Showing the church's then fitness for the great work that is committed to her, Inspiration continues: "Mighty miracles were wrought the sick were healed, and signs and wonders followed the believers."—*Early Writings*, p. 278.

As these mighty works are done in the time of the "Loud Cry of the Third Angel's Message," the purification, therefore, incontrovertibly takes place at the commencement of the "Loud Cry." And from this it follows as a logical necessity that Ezekiel's prophecy of marking and slaying must contain the announcement of the purification of the church.

Continuing to behold in vision the cherubim and the glory of God's throne, the prophet saw the Lord come to the threshold of the house (church), and as He gave charge to His angel who was "clothed with linen" and who "had the writer's inkhorn by his side," Ezekiel heard Him command the man: "Go through the midst of the city, through the midst of Jerusalem, and set a mark upon the foreheads of the men that sigh and that cry for all the abominations that be done in the midst thereof.

"And to the others He said in mine hearing, Go ye after him through the city, and smite: let not your eye spare, neither have ye pity: Slay utterly old and young, both maids and little children, and women: but come not near any man upon whom is the mark; and begin at My sanctuary. Then they began at the ancient men which were before the house. And He said unto them, Defile the house, and fill the courts with the slain: go ye forth. And they went forth and slew in the *city.*

"And it came to pass, while they were slaying them, and I was left, that I fell upon my face, and cried, and said, Ah Lord God! Wilt Thou destroy all the residue of *Israel* in Thy pouring out of Thy fury upon *Jerusalem?* Then said He unto me, The iniquity of the *house of Israel* and *Judah* is exceeding great, and the land is full of blood, and the city full of perverseness: for they say, The Lord hath forsaken the earth, and the Lord seeth not." Ezek. 9:3-9.

Revealing a complete separation of the *wicked from* among the *just*, these verses, therefore, prophetically forewarn of the imminent purification of the church— her only salvation. And taking place in "the city," "Jerusalem," "Israel," and "Judah,"

—terms by none of which the world can be called, as they apply exclusively to the people of God, the church,—this work of separation is, accordingly, confined strictly to the church.

The fact, furthermore, that the *wicked* are taken *from* among the righteous, also shows that the separation cannot be in the world. Were it there, it would have to be done in the opposite way—the *righteous* be taken *from* among the *wicked*.

Remember that the Lord said to Ezekiel: "Son of man, I send thee to the *children of Israel*, to a rebellious nation that hath rebelled against Me." "For thou art *not sent* to a *people* of a *strange speech* and of an hard language, *but to the house of Israel*" (Ezek. 2:3; 3:5) —a mission which is to result in

The Sealing of the 144,000—The First Fruits.

"This mightiest of angels," says the Spirit of Prophecy, "has in his hand the seal of the living God, or of Him who alone can give life, who can inscribe upon the foreheads the mark. . . ."

"This sealing of the servants of God is the *same* that was shown to Ezekiel in vision. John also had been a witness of this *most startling revelation*."—*Testimonies to Ministers*, pp. 444, 445.

The sealing (Rev. 7) being the same as the marking (Ezek. 9),—the "*purification*",

—we thus are given a twofold view of the "closing work for the church, . . . *the sealing time of the one hundred and forty-four thousand* who are to stand without fault before the throne of God. . . . They feel most deeply the *wrongs of God's professed people*. This is forcibly set forth by the prophet's illustration of the last work under the figure of the men each having a slaughter weapon in his hand. One man among them was clothed with linen, with a writer's inkhorn by his side."—*Testimonies*, Vol. 3, p. 266.

Since the purification, or the sealing, came at the commencement of the "Loud Cry," as we have already seen, the 144,000 are therefore the "first-fruits"—the first to be sealed; whereas those who are sealed after the purification of the church, are the second fruits, of whom John (after having seen the 144,000 sealed) says: "*After this* I beheld, and, lo, a great multitude, which no man could number, of all nations, and kindreds, and people, and tongues, stood before the throne, and before the Lamb, clothed with white robes, and palms in their hands." Rev. 7:9.

The fact therefore that there is an ingathering of two fruits, shows that the marking or sealing is in two sections—two periods—and that there are

Two Sealing Reports.

"And behold," says Ezekiel, "the man clothed with linen, which had the inkhorn by his side, *reported* the matter [*while on earth*], saying, I have done as Thou hast commanded me." Ezek. 9:11. Here is the first report, made at the completion of the sealing in the church—the sealing of the first-fruits, the 144,000.

"I saw," says the servant of the Lord, ". . . an angel with a writer's inkhorn by his side returned *from the earth,* and *reported* to Jesus that his work was done, and the saints were numbered and sealed."—*Early Writings*, p. 279. Here is his second report, made at the completion of the sealing in the world—the sealing of the second fruits, the great multitude.

Comparing both reports, each is seen to be of a different event: At the first report, the Lord was on "the *threshold* of the *house*" on *earth* (Ezek. 9:3); at the second, He was in the *heavenly sanctuary.*

After the angel had made his first report, the Lord commanded him: "Go in between the wheels, even under the cherub, and fill thine hand with coals of fire from between the cherubims, and scatter them over the city. And he went in in my sight." Ezek. 10:2.

But following his second report, ". . . all the angelic host laid off their crowns as Jesus made the solemn declaration, 'He that is unjust, let him be unjust still; and he which is filthy, let him be filthy still; and he that is righteous, let him be righteous still; and he that is holy, let him be holy still.' "—*Early Writings*, pp. 279, 280.

Were probation to close at the time of the *first report* (Ezek. 9:11), the Lord must, according to the foregoing statement, be in heaven, then descend to earth to receive His saints, instead of being already on earth, then mounting up in His throne, as He actually does, without His saints (Ezek. 10:19).

Again: the prophet's being left behind when the Lord went up, figuratively shows that at this particular descent and ascent, the saints are not to be taken to heaven, but only to be set free from sin and sinners—fitted for the final work.

At the angel's *second report*, however, Jesus, being in heaven, "*moved out* of the most holy place" (*Early Writings*, p. 280) to descend to earth.

This brief comparison brings into primary focus the twofold fact that at the time of the first report, Jesus went *into* the temple, whereas at the time of the second report, He went *out*.

Beyond the angel's reporting the matter of the marking and slaying in the church Ezekiel was not given to see. But Isaiah was. He saw

The Escaped Ones Go to All Nations.

"For by fire and by His sword," declares

the gospel prophet, "will the Lord plead with all flesh: and the slain of the Lord shall be many. . . . And I will send those that escape of them unto the nations, . . . to the isles afar off, that have not heard My fame, neither have seen My glory; and they shall declare My glory among the Gentiles. And they shall bring all your brethren for an offering unto the Lord out of all nations . . . to My holy mountain Jerusalem, saith the Lord, . . . *in a clean vessel into the house of the Lord.*" Isa. 66:16, 19, 20.

Since "those that escape" the slaughter (the 144,000) shall "bring *all* your brethren [all those who shall be saved in the time of the 'Loud Cry'] . . . into the house of the Lord," then it follows that those who escape are the ones who finish the work—the reason they are called "the servants of God." Rev. 7:3.

The message, moreover, finding them in the church, not in the world, they are therefore "virgins;" that is, "not defiled with women" (Rev. 14:4)—the churches of the world. And they are without guile in their mouths, having kept their tongues from

Criticising and Faultfinding.

". . . They will question and criticise everything" says the Spirit of Prophecy in forewarning of the purification, "that arises in the *unfolding of truth*, criticise the work and position of others, criticize

—23—

every branch of the work in which *they have not themselves* a part. They will feed upon the errors and mistakes and faults of others, 'until,' *said the angel*, 'the Lord Jesus shall rise up *from* his mediatorial work in the heavenly sanctuary, and shall clothe himself with the garments of vengeance, and surprise them at their unholy feast; and they will find themselves unprepared for the marriage supper of the Lamb.' "—*Testimonies*, Vol. 5, p. 690.

These solemn words, may each lay well to heart, and may none let the enemy beguile them "with good words and fair speeches" on this life-and-death matter. Fix in your mind the fact that Christ's rising "up from His mediatorial work" cannot be after probation has closed, for, note carefully, He is to "rise up" during "the *unfolding of truth*."

Let each take heed that he fall not to criticizing the message or messengers, but rather that he "sigh and cry," as the Lord bids, "for all the abominations that be done in the midst [the church]," lest he be found on the wrong side, ranged with the evildoers, and thus doomed to fall under the angels' slaughter weapons.

"Cry aloud, spare not," is the heartening order, "lift up thy voice like a trumpet, and *shew* My people their transgression, and the house of Jacob their sins." Isa. 58:1. Take your stand, Brother, Sister, on the right side, and make sure, "having done all, to stand," for, no escaping the fact, the Lord has set His hand to separate "the wicked *from among* the just," as is further seen

In the Light of The Parables.

"And when the king came in to see the guests, he saw there a man which had not on a wedding garment: ... Then said the king to the servants, Bind him hand and foot, and *take him away*, and cast him into outer darkness; there shall be weeping and gnashing of teeth." Matt. 22:11, 13.

This investigating and casting out takes place before probation closes, for the marriage ceremony had not yet been performed at the time that the "king came in to see the guests."

"Again, the kingdom of heaven is like unto a net, that was cast into the sea, and gathered of every kind: which, when it was full, they drew to shore, and sat down, and gathered the good into vessels, but cast the bad away. So shall it be at the end of the world: the angels shall come forth, and sever the wicked *from* among the just, and shall cast them into the furnace of fire: there shall be wailing and gnashing of teeth." Matt. 13:47-50.

In this scripture, too, is seen the purification of the church, for the bad ones are taken away *from among the good*, and *not the* good *from among the bad*; that is, the bad that are in the net (church) are thrown out, and the good ones kept.

This net represents the gospel work up to the time of the purification of the church, for after the church has been purified, only such as "should be saved" will be granted membership: "Awake, awake; put on thy strength, O Zion; *put* on thy beautiful garments, O Jerusalem, the holy city: for *henceforth* there shall no more come into thee the *uncircumcised* and the *unclean.*" Isa. 52:1.

This rousing alarm must sound before probation closes, for it could do no good afterwards, indeed could be but a mockery then. Neither could it apply to the time of the "Loud Cry," for the church is not then asleep and without the "beautiful garments": "Only those," confirms the Spirit of Prophecy, "who have withstood and overcome temptation in the strength of the Mighty One will be permitted to act a part in proclaiming this message when it shall have swelled into the Loud Cry."—*Review and Herald,* Nov. 19, 1908. "And in that day there shall be *no more* the *Canaanite* in the house of the Lord of hosts." Zech. 14:21.

"And the *Gentiles* shall see thy righteousness, and *all kings thy glory*: and thou shalt be called by a new name, which the mouth of the Lord shall name." Isa. 62:2. "Therefore thy gates shall be open continually; they shall not be shut day nor night;

that men may bring unto thee the forces of the Gentiles, and that their kings may be brought." Isa. 60:11.

In the purification of the church, "the angels shall . . . sever the *wicked from among the just*" (Matt. 13:49), but in the time of the "Loud Cry," they shall gather the *just from among the wicked.* So it is written: "And after these things I saw another angel come down from heaven, having great power; and the earth was lightened with his glory. . . . And I heard another voice from heaven, saying, *Come out* of her, *My people*, that ye be not partakers of her sins, and that ye receive not of her plagues." Rev. 18:1, 4.

These two distinct separations, each at a different time, occur when (to recapitulate the facts specifically), in the time of the firstfruits, the wicked are taken from among the righteous in the church (net), and when, in the time of the second fruits, the righteous are taken from among the wicked in Babylon. And such a church— pure in the absolute—presupposes an absolutely

Pure Message.

Ezekiel's prophecy revealing itself to be a message for the church today, the prophet, himself, must necessarily, then, represent the messengers who carry the message to the church at the time appointed. And in response to the Lord's command, "Be not thou rebellious like that rebellious house: open thy mouth, and eat that I give thee," Ezekiel's reply, "Then did I eat it; and it was in my mouth *as honey* for sweetness" (Ezek. 2:8; 3:3), shows that the messengers obey the Lord and love His Word above everything else.

"And I," said the Lord, "will make thy tongue cleave to the roof of thy mouth, that thou shalt be *dumb*, . . . But *when* I speak with thee, I *will open thy mouth*, and thou shalt say unto them, Thus saith the *Lord God;* He that heareth, let him hear; and he that forbeareth, let him forbear: for they are a rebellious house." Ezek. 3:26, 27.

This positive declaration by the Lord, Himself, manifests that the message be unadulterated—the pure truth, proof absolute against contamination of man's utterance. The messengers, being made *dumb*, can speak only when He opens their mouths, and only what He puts in their mouths—a "Thus saith the Lord God." Taking no credit to themselves, they are to

Exalt Inspiration.

"If any man," says the Apostle Paul, "think himself to be a prophet, or spiritual, let him acknowledge that the things that I write unto you are the commandments of the Lord." 1 Cor. 14:37.

When God speaks through a person, that one, as His mouthpiece, must acknowledge the fact, lest there overtake him a fate similar to that which befell Herod, who, "upon a set day . . . , arrayed in royal apparel, sat upon his throne, and made an oration unto them. And the people gave a shout, saying, It is the voice of a god, and not of a man. And immediately the angel of the Lord smote him, because he gave not God the glory: and he was eaten of worms, and gave up the ghost." Acts 12:21-23.

From this dreadful experience, recorded for our warning, and from the other grave truths brought forth herein, we plainly see that in order for the Lord to prepare His servants for the seal, He is setting forth every necessary lesson, even the lesson inherent in

The Way the Message is Derived.

The reader will note that, though the prophet was bidden to go speak to his people, yet instead of being told what to say, he was commanded: "Open thy mouth, and eat that I give thee. And when I looked," says Ezekiel, "behold, an hand was sent unto me; and, lo, a roll of a book was therein. . . . Moreover he said unto me, Son of man, eat that thou findest; eat this roll, and go speak unto the house of Israel. So I opened my mouth, and he caused me to eat that roll." Ezek. 2:8, 9; 3:1, 2.

As the words which Ezekiel was to speak to his people were found in the book which he ate, the "book" can be none other than the *Bible*, from which comes the message culminating in

Joy, Mourning, and Woe.

"And, lo, a roll of a book was therein; and he spread it before me; and it was written *within* and *without*: and there was written therein *lamentations*, and *mourning*, and *woe*" (Ezek. 2:9, 10)—dire writ envisaging the slaughter in Ezekiel 9, and the woes pronounced in the Master's parables: "The Lord of that servant shall come in a day when he looketh not for Him, and in an hour that he is not aware of. And shall cut him asunder, and appoint him his portion with the hypocrites: there shall be weeping and gnashing of teeth." "Then said the king to the servants, Bind him hand and foot, and take him away, and cast him into outer darkness; there shall be weeping and gnashing of teeth." Matt. 24:50, 51; 22:13.

And aforetime through His servant Moses, He declared unto His people: "It shall come to pass, if thou wilt not hearken unto the voice of the Lord thy God, to observe to do all His commandments and His statutes which I command thee this day; that all these curses shall come upon thee, and overtake thee." Deut. 28:15. "I call heaven and earth to record this day against you, that I have set before you life and death, blessing and cursing: therefore choose life, that both thou and thy seed may live." Deut. 30:19.

The "book" which Ezekiel ate being "written within and without" (Ezek. 2:10), the writing "within," therefore, can only be the prophetic Word of God, proclaiming the curses and the blessings that are written in the Bible; while the writing "without," can be nothing else but the sure record of the fulfillment of that within—the record, in short, of the prophecy's becoming history; showing thereby that God has spoken it and will perform it.

The writing "within and without," moreover, signifies also that the message will be in type and antitype.

When Ezekiel *ate* the "book," it was, as is also to be noted, in his mouth "as *honey* for sweetness," but *not* "bitter" in his "belly," as was the one which John ate (Rev 10:10). Though, therefore, as the Word shows, there will be no disappointment with this message, as there was with the one in 1844 A.D., yet, sadly, it declares that to its warning, the people to whom it is sent

Will Stop Their Ears and Close Their Doors.

"But the house of Israel will not hearken unto thee; for they will not hearken unto Me: for *all* the house of Israel are impudent and hardhearted." Ezek. 3:7. "But thou, O son of man, behold, they shall put bands upon thee, and shall bind thee with them, and thou shalt *not go* out among them: . . . and shalt not be to them a reprover: for they are a rebellious house." Ezek. 3:25, 26.

"In the last solemn work," predicts the Spirit of Prophecy in identical view, "few great men will be engaged."—*Testimonies*, Vol. 5, p. 80. ". . . they will not recognize the work of God when the loud cry of the third angel shall be heard. When light goes forth to lighten the earth, instead of coming up to the help of the Lord, they will want to bind about His work to meet their narrow ideas. . . . There will be those among us who will always want to control the work of God, to dictate even what movements shall be made when the work goes forward under the direction of the angel who joins the third angel in the message to be given to the world."—*Testimonies to Ministers*, p. 300. Hence the question:

How Will the Message Reach the People?

On account of their refusing to hear, "God will use ways and means," answers the Spirit of Prophecy, "by which it will be seen that He is taking the reins in His own hands. The workers will be surprised by the simple means that He will use to bring about and perfect His work of righteousness."—*Id.*, p. 300.

"God has promised that where the shepherds are not true he will *take charge* of the flock himself. . . . In this time, the gold will be separated from the dross in the church. True godliness will be clearly distinguished from the appearance and tinsel of it. Many a star that we have admired for its brilliancy, will then go out in darkness. . . . Those who have been timid and self-distrustful, will declare themselves openly for Christ and his truth. The most weak and hesitating in the church, will be as David—willing to do and dare" (*Testimonies*, Vol. 5, pp. 80, 81)—facts which, along with those which ensue, show that

Nothing Can Hinder the Lord.

Glancing at the cover-page objectification the reader will note that "two wings of every one" of the living creatures "were joined one to another." Ezek. 1:11. Both they and the wheels, therefore, each formed a square: "one wheel by one cherub, and another wheel by another cherub." Ezek. 10:9.

As Ezekiel viewed the creatures approaching, he saw that they had "the face of a man" in the front, "the face of an eagle" in the back, "the face of a lion on the right side," and the "face of an ox on the left side" (Ezek. 1:10), for they four had "four sides" (verse 8); also that they had wings, "two . . . on this side, and . . . two . . . on that side" (verse 23). He saw the living wheels, moreover, so arranged that "they went upon their four sides." Ezek. 1:17. (See cover-page.)

The four-way vision of the living creatures, along with the four-way movement of the wheels, enables four-directional motion—forward or backward, to the right or to the left: the living creatures "turned not as they went." Ezek. 10:11.

"And their feet "being "straight feet" (Ezek. 1:7), it enabled them to move freely in any direction without turning, so that they "ran and returned as the appearance of a flash of lightning" (Verse 14). "And the glory of the God of Israel was over them above" (Ezek. 10:19), "and the likeness of the hands of a man was under their wings." Verse 21.

As these wheels, making a square formation, "ran and returned," and as "over them above," God was sitting on His throne, it is evident that this marvelous living mechanism is the vehicle of God—His chariot in which He has come to bring the message to separate the "wicked from among the just." Thus is animated the solemnity that as the "battle is the Lord's," verily "He will take charge of the flock Himself."

"As the wheel-like complications were under the guidance of the hand beneath the wings of the cherubim, so the complicated play of human events is under divine control. Amidst the strife and tumult of nations, He that sitteth above the cherubim still guides the affairs of this earth.

"The history of nations speaks to us today. To every nation and to every individual

God has assigned a place in His great plan. Today men and nations are being tested by the plummet in the hand of Him who makes no mistake. All are by their own choice deciding their destiny, and God is overruling all for the accomplishment of His purposes."—*Prophets and Kings*, p. 536.

"In Ezekiel's vision, God had his hand beneath the wings of the cherubim. This is to teach his servants that it is divine power that gives them success. He will work with them if they will put away iniquity, and become pure in heart and life.

"The bright light going among the living creatures with the swiftness of lightning represents the speed with which this work will finally go forward to completion" in behalf of His people during the Judgment hour (*Testimonies*, Vol. 5, p. 754): for the faces of the living creatures are

Figurative of the Saints in Time of Judgment.

The faces of the cherubim being the same as those of the beasts of the Revelation, they both necessarily have complementary significance, the key to which John supplies: "And they sung a new song, saying, Thou art worthy to take the book, and to open the seals thereof: for thou wast slain, and hast *redeemed us* to God by *Thy blood* out of *every kindred*, and *tongue*, and *people*, and *nation*." Rev. 5:9.

The very fact that these beasts have been redeemed by the blood of Christ and shall reign upon earth, shows that they are symbolical of the saints, even as the beasts of Daniel are symbolical of the nations. Necessarily, then, the faces of the cherubim, just as with the faces of the beasts standing before the Judgment throne, are figurative of the saints in time of Judgment.

The Lord's being "over them [the cherubim] above," signifies that this is the living chariot in which He, their Saviour, is subsequently to translate the saints.

And "on each side of the cloudy chariot," echoes the Spirit of Prophecy, "were wings, and beneath it were living wheels; and as the chariot rolled upward, the wheels cried, 'Holy,' and the wings, as they moved, cried, 'Holy,' and the retinue of holy angels around the cloud cried, 'Holy holy, holy, Lord God Almighty!' and the saints in the cloud cried 'Glory! Alleluia!' "—*Early Writings*, p. 287.

That the all-happy hour is approaching when we shall mount up in this most glorious chariot, so stirs our hearts as to cause us fairly to shout the questions:

When Will This Chariot Arrive? How Long Will It Stay?

When considered in the light of the four main facts so far established, these questions are virtually self-answering: (1) the

Lord comes to earth in this chariot; (2) from it He commands Ezekiel to go speak to His people; (3) Ezekiel did not bear the message to the people of his day; (4) he will bear it to the people at the commencement of the "Loud Cry."

Thus it is seen that when the time comes that the church has reached the condition described by the Lord (Ezek. 3-9), the mystery of the vision is to be revealed, and the message carried to the church. And that the church has already reached this time and condition is conclusively evidenced by the threefold fact that the first part of this "most startling revelation" (dilated herein), was published in December, 1930, in a 255-page book entitled *The Shepherd's Rod*, Vol.1; that the second part was published in the month of September, 1932, in a 304-page book entitled *The Shepherd's Rod*, Vol. 2; and that the third part—the series of tracts (of which this is the first) which since 1933 aggregates to date some 898 pages—comprises Volume 3.

The fact, therefore, that from the chariot, the Lord commands the prophet to go speak, bear the message, to His people, and that the message totals over 1250 pages of literature published since 1930, unfolding its truth from different angles, solemnly reveals that the chariot, though invisible to human beings (as to "the young man" were the chariots which covered the mountains—2 Kings 6:17), has already arrived.

And since it is already here, it must of course be the divine instrumentality through which, as a sort of base of operations, the Lord is ordering and directing His work, and through which He shall do so until "this gospel of the kingdom . . . be preached in all the world for a witness unto all nations; and . . . the end come." Matt. 24:14. "The end"—the unbelievable! to those who say, "Where is the promise of His coming? for since the fathers fell asleep, all things continue as they were from the beginning of the creation" (2 Pet. 3:4); but the long-looked-for, to those who shall say, "Lo, this is our God; we have waited for Him, and He will save us" (Isa. 25:9). — Dreadful, awful, finality! it should drive all to ascertain

The Purpose of the Message.

"And it came to pass, while they were slaying them, and I was left, that I fell upon my face, and cried, and said, Ah Lord God! wilt Thou destroy all the residue of Israel in Thy pouring out of Thy fury upon Jerusalem? Then said He unto me, The iniquity of the house of Israel and Judah is exceeding great, . . . and as for Me also, Mine eye shall not spare, neither will I have pity." Ezek. 9:8-10.

After the sighing and crying ones were marked (which is not to be understood as being consummated in its entirety world-wide before the slaying follows anywhere), the slaughter completed, and the matter reported, the Lord "spake unto the man clothed with linen, and said, Go in between the wheels, even under the cherub, and fill thine hand with coals of fire from between the cherubims, and scatter them over the city." Ezek. 10:2.

The scattering of the "coals of fire . . . over the city" represents absolute purification of the heart (*Gospel Workers*, p. 23) effected by the outpouring of the Holy Spirit upon those who receive the "mark"—those who escape the "slaughter."

Following the completion of the "slaughter," and just preceding the scattering of the "coals of fire" "over the city," "the cherubims stood on the right side of the house, . . . and the cloud filled the inner court." Ezek. 10:2, 3. Later they "lifted up their wings, and mounted up from the earth in my sight," says the prophet. Ezek. 10:19. Then subsequently he saw them again "lift up their wings" (Ezek. 11:22, 23), showing that though they had departed after the separation took place (10:3, 19), they had later returned, and were now departing for the second time.

With the city thus purged of sin and sinners, and none but the "residue," the righteous, remaining, "I, saith the Lord, will be unto her a wall of fire round about, and will be the glory in the midst of her. . . . Sing and rejoice, O daughter of Zion: for, lo, I come, and I will dwell in the midst of thee, saith the Lord. And many nations shall be joined to the Lord in that day, and shall be My people: and I will dwell in the midst of thee, and thou shalt know that the Lord of hosts hath sent me unto thee." Zech. 2:5, 10, 11. (For a more ample explanation of these verses, see *The Shepherd's Rod*, Vol. 2, pp. 259-282.)

Mark that while He dwells in the midst of His people, "many nations shall be joined to the Lord *in that day*," and that He will be unto them "a wall of fire round about." Here we are graphically reassured that "in that day," in the day that the Lord takes the reins in His Own hands and comes to dwell in the midst of the city, His Presence, His marvelous chariot, shall be a protection round about His people!

Thus it is seen that the Lord has come to purify His people by putting away the wicked from among them, "take charge" of His *clean flock*, and with them finish His work. In this we see that the church has come to her crisis. She that travaileth "must give birth." And "as soon as Zion travailed, she brought forth her children." Isa. 66:8.

Then shall the chariot, being dedicated to the saints, and filled to capacity, take off for the portals of glory—"the land that is very far off." ". . . and as the chariot rolled upward, the wheels cried, 'Holy,' and the wings, as they moved, cried, 'holy,' and the retinue of holy angels *around* the cloud cried, 'Holy, holy, holy, Lord God

Almighty!' And the saints in the cloud cried, 'Glory! Alleluia!' And the chariot rolled upward to the holy city."—*Early Writings*, pp. 287, 288.

In view of this glorious prospect, along with the overawing magnitude and majesty of the work before us, and the exceeding shortness of the time in which to accomplish it, let each hasten to share of

The Responsibility of Those Who Bear the Message.

Since Ezekiel represents those whose hearts the message has reached, then to them the Lord is speaking when He says: "Son of man, I have made thee a watchman unto the house of Israel: therefore hear the word at My mouth, and give them warning from Me. When I say unto the wicked, Thou shalt surely die; and thou givest him not warning, nor speakest to warn the wicked from his wicked way, to save his life; the same wicked man shall die in his iniquity; but his blood will I require at thine hand. Yet if thou warn the wicked, and he turn not from his wickedness, nor from his wicked way, he shall die in his iniquity; but thou hast delivered thy soul.

"Again, When a righteous man doth turn from his righteousness, and commit iniquity, and I lay a stumbling block before him, he shall die: because thou hast not given him warning, he shall die in his sin, and his righteousness which he hath done shall not be remembered; but his blood will I require at thine hand. Nevertheless if thou warn the righteous man, that the righteous sin not, and he doth not sin, he shall surely live, because he is warned; also thou hast delivered thy soul." Ezek. 3:17-21.

Because of the unfaithfulness of the former watchmen, the Lord makes the anti-typical Ezekiel—he and she who "sigh and cry for the abominations that be done in the midst thereof" (the church) —a "watchman" (Ezek. 3:17) in their stead. Be careful, therefore, Brother, Sister, lest you also betray your trust and find yourself thrust out. "Wherefore let him that thinketh he standeth take heed lest he fall." 1 Cor. 10:12. Only those who thus humble themselves now, will the Lord exalt in due time to be

His Faithful Watchmen to Stand Before the Unfaithful.

"Those who have trusted to intellect, genius, or talent, will not then stand at the head of rank and file. They *did not* keep pace with the light. Those who have proved themselves unfaithful will not then be entrusted with the flock. In the *last solemn* work *few* great men will be engaged. They are self-sufficient, independent of God, and he cannot use them."—*Testimonies*, Vol. 5, p. 80.

"The Lord's servants will be called enthusiasts. Ministers will warn the people not to listen to them. Noah received the same treatment while the Spirit of God was urging him to give the message. . . ."— *Testimonies to Ministers*, p. 233.

The fact that our conferences grant ministerial licenses only to college-trained men, attests that they are trusting to "intellect, genius, and talent." "God's watchmen will not cry, 'Peace, peace,' when God has not spoken peace. The voice of the faithful watchmen will be heard: 'Go ye out from hence, touch not the unclean. . . . Be ye clean that bear the vessels of the Lord.' "—*Testimonies*, Vol. 5, p. 83.

Receive instruction and learn to obey the word of the Lord, for in so doing He will enable you to do great things in His name. Incline your ear and hear the Lord's heartening assurance: "Behold I have made thy face strong against their faces, and thy forehead strong against their foreheads. As an adamant harder than flint have I made thy forehead: fear them not, neither be dismayed at their looks, though they be a rebellious house. . . . all My words that I shall speak unto thee receive in thine heart, and hear with thine ears. And go, get thee to them . . . and speak unto them, and tell them, Thus saith the Lord God; whether they will hear, or whether they will forbear." Ezek. 3:8-11.

Beyond this, the Spirit-controlled movement of the chariot shows that the Spirit is to be the all-controlling power: for "whithersoever the spirit was to go, they [the living creatures] went, thither was their spirit to go; and the wheels were lifted up over against them: for the spirit of the living creature was in the wheels." Ezek. 1:20.

"As never before, we should pray not only that laborers may be sent forth into the great harvest-field, but that we may have a clear conception of truth, so that when the messengers of truth shall come, we may accept the message and respect the messenger."— *Testimonies*, Vol. 6, p. 420. Let us, therefore, sanctify the Lord of hosts Himself, and

Cease From Men.

As you will find yourself under severe trial if you obey your inner convictions and take hold of the truth, you must therefore let the Lord alone be your guide, and Inspiration your only teacher. Do not value your salvation so little as to trust to the wisdom of another. Be wise: obey the word of the Lord, investigate for yourself, and do not delay, for you know not the narrow margin of time between you and heaven! "Trust ye not in a friend, put ye not confidence in a guide: keep the doors of thy mouth from her that lieth in thy bosom." Mic. 7:5.

The rulers of ancient Israel—priests, scribes and pharisees—who deprived the people of their God-given right to investigate for themselves the teaching of Christ, perished along with their victims under the condemnation of the laws which were to save them.

"Woe unto you, lawyers!" therefore said Christ, "for ye have taken away the key of knowledge: ye entered not in yourselves, and them that were entering in ye hindered." Luke 11:52.

This fatal mistake was repeated during the Reformation, also in the preaching of the First, Second, and Third Angels' messages. Thus each one who accepted the advancing truth and became a member of the Seventh-day Adventist denomination, did so only by making his own investigation and decision independently of priest or scribe or pharisee. And if that method of investigation was the only sane and safe one then, it is just as certainly so now when we understand God's Word better than when we first believed! And though for your following obediently in the way God commands, the unfaithful watchmen of today "cast you out," and remove your name from the church books, you should rejoice (Isa. 66:5; Luke 6:22, 23), and gladly endure the trial of your faith, knowing that it "worketh for us a far more exceeding and eternal weight of glory" (2 Cor. 4:17); that, indeed, your accepting the truth and obeying it is the only thing that will forever insure your membership with the redeemed, in the church eternal, and that the only book that is worth-while having your name in is "The Lamb's Book of Life."

"The people accept their ministers' explanations of Scripture, and do not investigate for themselves. Therefore by working through the ministers," says Satan, "I can control the people according to my will."—*Testimonies to Ministers*, p. 473. Thus because of "those who . . . have confidence in the leading men, and accept the decisions they make; . . . many will reject the very messages God sends to His people, if these leading brethren do not accept them."—*Id.*, pp. 106, 107. ". . . if they carry their opposition so far as to oppose that in which they have had no experience, . . . the church may know that they are not right."—*Testimonies*, Vol. 5, pp. 668, 669.

"Behold, to obey is better than sacrifice, and to hearken than the fat of rams." I Sam. 15:22.

"And it shall come to pass at that time, that I will search Jerusalem with candles, and punish the men that are settled on their lees: that say in their heart, The Lord will not do good, neither will He do evil." Zeph. 1:12.

"And He shall sit as a refiner and purifier of silver: and He shall purify the sons of Levi, and purge them as gold and silver, that they may offer unto the Lord an offering in righteousness." Mal. 3:3.

He "Whose fan is in His hand, . . . will throughly purge His floor, and gather His wheat into the garner; but He will burn up the chaff with unquenchable fire." Matt. 3:12.

"And they that be wise shall shine as the brightness of the firmament; and they that turn many to righteousness as the stars for ever and ever." Dan. 12:3.

"Cry aloud," therefore, and "spare not, lift up thy voice like a trumpet, and shew My people their transgression, and the house of Jacob their sins." Isa. 58:1.

"Behold upon the mountains the feet of Him that bringeth good tidings, that publisheth peace! O Judah, keep thy solemn feasts, perform thy vows: for the wicked shall no more pass through thee; he is utterly cut off." Nah. 1:15.

". . . the Lord of hosts mustereth the host of the battle." Isa. 13:4.

"The Lord's voice crieth unto the city, and the man of wisdom shall see thy name: hear ye the rod, and Who hath appointed it." Mic. 6:9.

"For as the rain cometh down, and the snow from heaven, and returneth not thither, but watereth the earth, and maketh it bring forth and bud, that it may give seed to the sower, and bread to the eater: So shall My word be that goeth forth out of My mouth: it shall not return unto Me void, but it shall accomplish that which I please, and it shall prosper in the thing whereto I sent it." Isa. 55:10, 11.

"But beware of rejecting that which is truth. The great danger with our people has been that of depending upon men, and making flesh their arm."—*Testimonies to Ministers*, p. 106.

"For Zion's sake will I not hold My peace, and for Jerusalem's sake I will not rest, until the righteousness thereof go forth as brightness, and the salvation thereof as a lamp that burneth." Isa. 62:1.

O my ministering brethren, though you have hardened your hearts against the message and have steadfastly refused to "hearken" to it, yet God is still pleading with you to surrender before it is too late. Thus this

Second Appeal and Prayer.

Though you have unrighteously ignored the Lord's written appeal placed in your hands at the General Conference convention in 1930, and have obdurately turned your eyes and your steps away from the additional light of the "Three Angels' Messages," yet even more unrighteously you broadcasted (before the meeting with us by the "Conference investigating committee," on February 19, 1934, at Los Angeles, California) throughout the denomination the false report that you had given us a hearing. But despite this misrepresentation, God still loves you, and we still love you, and He will forgive you and hold nothing against you if you will penitently ask Him to.

(Before the first edition of this tract was published, they had not given us any hearing. But since then they have. But that it was worse than none at all, is seen from the faithful report in our Tract No. 7, *Count the Evidences on Both Sides Before Firing for or Against*.)

My words being generally misconstrued, and carrying apparently but little weight with some, my prayer, therefore, shall be from the Scriptures, and my appeal from the Spirit of Prophecy. Surely, my brethren, you will take heed to the Words of God:

"Lord, I have loved the habitation of Thy house, and the place where Thine honour dwelleth." Ps. 26:8. And ". . . the zeal of Thine house hath eaten me up; and the reproaches of them that reproached Thee are fallen upon me." "It was not an enemy that reproached me; . . . but it was . . . a man mine equal, my guide, . . . *we . . . walked unto the house of God in company.*" Ps. 69:9, 55:12, 13, 14. Therefore "save us, O God of our salvation, and *gather us together*, and deliver us from the heathen, that we may give thanks to Thy holy name, and glory in Thy praise." 1 Chron. 16:35.

"Come now, and let us reason together, saith the Lord: though your sins be as scarlet, they shall be as white as snow; though they be red like crimson, they shall be as wool." Isa. 1:18. "Anoint thine eyes with eyesalve, that thou mayest see." Rev. 3:18.

Your attitude, my brethren, toward the glorious light now shining upon the "Three Angels' Messages," is but a fulfillment of prophecy: "Because thou sayest, I am rich, and increased with goods, and have need of nothing",—truth or prophets,—you refuse to be interested in investigating the cry of the Angel whose glory is to "lighten the earth."

"The light which will lighten the earth with its glory will be called a false light, by those who refuse to walk in its advancing glory."—*Review and Herald,* May 27, 1890.

"The prophet declares, "And after these things I saw an angel come down from heaven, having great power; and the earth was lightened with his glory.' Brightness, glory, and power are to be connected with the third angel's message, and conviction will follow wherever it is preached in demonstration of the Spirit. How will any of our brethren know when this light shall come to the people of God?"—*Review and Herald*, April 1, 1890.

You well know that the Truth, in which we have greatly rejoiced since 1844, has come through God's appointed servant whose writings we call the "Spirit of Prophecy." That voice is now speaking to you, anew, in this urgent appeal:

"Let no one come to the conclusion that there is no more truth to be revealed."—*Testimonies on Sabbath School Work*, p. 53. No one is to make up his mind "that the whole truth has been unfolded, and that the Infinite One has no more light for His people."—*Id.*, p. 60.

"'Philip findeth Nathanael, and saith unto him, We have found Him, of whom Moses in the law, and the prophets, did write, Jesus of Nazareth, the Son of Joseph. And Nathanael said unto him: Can there any good thing come out of Nazareth?' Prejudice and unbelief sprang up in the heart of Nathanael, but Philip did not try to combat it. He said, 'Come and see.' "—*Id.*, p. 63.

". . . if a message comes that you *do not understand, take pains* that you may hear the reasons the messenger may give, . . . for your position will not be shaken by coming in contact with error. There is no virtue or manliness in keeping up a continual warfare in the *dark*, closing your eyes lest you may see, closing your ears lest you may hear, hardening your heart in ignorance and unbelief lest you may have to *humble* yourselves and acknowledge that you have received light on some points of truth.

"To hold yourselves aloof from an investigation of truth is *not* the way to carry out the Saviour's injunction to 'search the Scriptures.' Is it digging for hidden treasures to call the results of some one's labor a mass of rubbish, and make no critical examination to see whether or not there are precious jewels of truth in the collection of thought which you condemn? . . . Thus it was that the Jews did in the days of Christ, and we are warned not to do as they did, and be led to choose darkness rather than light. . . . No one of those who imagine that they *know it all* is too old or too intelligent to learn from the humblest of the messengers of the living God."—*Id.,* pp. 65, 66.

"Precious light is to shine forth from the Word of God and let no one presume to dictate what shall or what shall not be brought before the people in the messages of enlightenment that He shall send, and so quench the Spirit of God. Whatever may be his position of authority, no one has a right to shut away the light from the people. When a message comes in the name of the Lord to His people, *no one may* excuse himself from an investigation of its claims. No one can afford to stand back in an attitude of indifference and self-confidence, and say: 'I know what is truth. I am satisfied with my position. I have set my stakes, and I will not be moved away from my position, whatever may come. I will not listen to the message of this messenger; for I know that it can not be truth.' It was from pursuing this very course that the popular churches were left in partial darkness, and that is why the messages of heaven have not reached them."—*Id.,* p.65.

O, Brethren, what excuse will you have if you refuse to hearken to this entreaty also? Will it vindicate your wisdom and save your soul if you find yourselves on the wrong side? If so, surely then you will want to make the most of it. But if not, then do make haste to get on the right side, even though it humble you to the dust to come to the Light. May you not say again: "He has taken the Testimonies out of their setting." May you cease trying to obstruct the way, that the message reach not the people, since you are warned: "Let no one presume to dictate what shall or what shall not be brought before the people in the messages of enlightenment that He shall send, and so quench the Spirit of God." God forbid!

(all italics ours)

———————

Though the subject matter of this tract could have been greatly enlarged, it has, for the sake of brevity, been thus compacted, carrying only the key points unlocking the message which is pleading at the doors of God's dear church. Whoever, therefore, has read this far, should let no obstacle prevent him from sending for all the

Free Literature.

The Present Truth series of publications reveal that "the days are at hand, and the effect of every vision" Ezek. 12:23); that is, the prophetic visions which appeared to be full of mysteries, are now become plain facts.

Address all orders to The Universal Publishing Association, P.O. Box 24027, Waco, Texas, 76702 U.S.A. or visit us on the web at UniversalPublishing. com.

". . . The Spirit of Truth, is come, He will guide you into all truth: for He shall not speak of Himself; but whatsoever He shall hear, that shall He speak: and He will shew you things to come." John 16:13.

SPIRIT OF PROPHECY INDEX

SCRIPTURAL INDEX

SCRIPTURAL INDEX—(Cont.)

—O—

TOPICAL INDEX